Developing embedded literacy, language and numeracy: supporting achievement

NIACE lifelines in adult learning

The *NIACE lifelines in adult learning* series provides straightforward background and information, accessible know-how and useful examples of good practice for all practitioners involved in adult and community learning. Focusing in turn on different areas of adult learning these guides are an essential part of every practitioner's toolkit.

1. **Community education and neighbourhood renewal** – Jane Thompson, ISBN 1 86201 139 7
2. **Spreading the word: reaching out to new learners** – Veronica McGivney, ISBN 1 86201 140 0
3. **Managing community projects for change** – Jan Eldred, ISBN 1 86201 141 9
4. **Engaging black learners in adult and community education** – Lenford White, ISBN 1 86201 142 7
5. **Consulting adults** – Chris Jude, ISBN 1 86201 194 4
6. **Working with young adults** – Carol Jackson, ISBN 1 86201 150 8
7. **Promoting learning** – Kate Malone, ISBN 1 86201 151 6
8. **Evaluating community projects** – Jane Field, ISBN 1 86201 152 4
9. **Working in partnership** – Lyn Tett, ISBN 1 86201 162 1
10. **Working with Asian heritage communities** – David McNulty, ISBN 1 86201 174 5
11. **Learning and community arts** – Tony Fegan, ISBN 1 86201 181 8
12. **Museums and community learning** – Garrick Fincham, ISBN 1 86201 182 6
13. **Developing a needs-based library service** – John Pateman, ISBN 1 86201 183 4
14. **Volunteers and volunteering** – Jan Eldred, ISBN 1 86201 187 7
15. **Sustaining projects for success** – Kay Snowdon, ISBN 1 86201 188 5
16. **Opening up schools for adults** – Judith Summers, ISBN 1 86201 192 3

Forthcoming titles

17. **Befriending learners** – Jane Field
18. **Developing literacy: supporting achievement** – Amanda Lindsay and Judith Gawn
19. **Developing numeracy: supporting achievement** – Barbara Newmarch
20. **Developing ESOL: supporting achievement** – Violet Windsor and Christina Healey
21. **Developing embedded literacy, language and numeracy: supporting achievement** – Jan Eldred
    The Jargon Buster – Yanina Dutton

21

Developing embedded literacy, language and numeracy: supporting achievement

Jan Eldred

The Regional Achievement Programme is
supported by the *Skills for Life* Strategy Unit

Published by the National Institute of
Adult Continuing Education (England and Wales)

21 De Montfort Street
Leicester LE1 7GE
Company registration no. 2603322
Charity registration no. 1002775

First published 2005

The *NIACE lifelines in adult learning series* is supported by the Adult
and Community Learning Fund. ACLF is funded by the Department
for Education and Skills and managed in partnership by NIACE and
the Basic Skills Agency to develop widening participation in adult learning.

niace
promoting adult learning

NIACE has a broad remit to promote lifelong learning
opportunities for adults. NIACE works to develop
increased participation in education and training,
particularly for those who do not have easy access
because of barriers of class, gender, age, race,
language and culture, learning difficulties and
disabilities, or insufficient financial resources.

www.niace.org.uk

Cataloguing in Publication Data
A CIP record of this title is available from the British Library

Designed and typeset by Boldface
Printed in Great Britain by Russell Press, Nottingham

ISBN 1 86201 219 9

Contents

Note to the reader

Inspirations: refer to case studies and examples of interesting practice.
Glossary: the meanings of the words underlined in the text can be
found in the glossary on page 44

Acknowledgements

Thanks are given to the groups and organisations which were part of the Developing Embedded Basic Skills (DEBS) research and development work, sponsored by ABSSU and LSC in 2002-2003. They formed the basis of insight into embedding basic skills and some are cited in this publication. Acknowledgment is made of the work of Heather Clary and Chris Taylor. Thanks are given to them for offering feedback on this publication.

The Regional Achievement Programme is supported by the *Skills for Life* Strategy Unit.

1 Introduction: Why does it matter?

Background

Since the beginning of the Adult Literacy Campaign of the 1970s the notion that literacy and numeracy should be taught within contexts which are relevant and purposeful to the learner has been paramount. While some teaching does, of necessity, demand an examination and exploration of the theory of literacy and numeracy, its application has, in good, responsive practice, responded to the interests and purposes of the individual. Discovery of why learners have sought to develop their skills and knowledge has been one of the key characteristics of provision and often provided a starting point for individual tuition. This approach is based on an understanding that literacy and numeracy are not only tools to function in society but also vehicles to engage with, make sense of and question, values and practices of living and working. The inclusion of English for Speakers of Other Languages (ESOL) in the umbrella term of basic skills is because literacy, language and numeracy (LLN) are seen as essential skills for living and working in the UK. They have some shared history and practices. Information and Communication Technology (ICT) is currently being considered as the fourth basic skill. Basic skills are currently being referred to as literacy, language and numeracy; some people refer to them as essential skills.

The delivery of LLN over the last 30 years has included a great deal of discrete provision. It has attracted many learners to colleges, community and work-based learning activities offered in small groups or one-to-one. However, the Moser report of 1999, *A Fresh Start*, suggested that few of the estimated seven million people, whose skills are not sufficiently developed, acknowledge they have any difficulties. The report claimed that:

> "Many people are unaware of their poor skills, and many, even if aware, don't regard it as a problem. And of course there is often a strong stigma in admitting to it." (DfEE, 1999, p21)

This suggests that some people have found ways of addressing any obstacles raised through poor skills, probably using other family members, close colleagues or avoidance strategies. For a wide range of reasons, these individuals are unlikely to seek out literacy, language and numeracy learning opportunities. Providers and practitioners are charged with finding different ways to help individuals develop their skills. Embedding LLN could offer this opportunity.

Embedding harnesses the way we use LLN

Embedding LLN is important because it harnesses the ways we use these skills. All social and economic activities, whether they are daily transactions at home or work or ground-breaking initiatives, involve LLN. Living and working, being part of a family, community, workplace, faith group, sports or social club, demand the use of LLN. Embedding approaches to teaching and learning use the purposes to which LLN will be put and capitalise on their natural associations.

Embedding helps to motivate learners

The Moser report also suggested that one of the most difficult challenges in developing a strategy to develop basic skills was to motivate people to become involved in learning:

"How to make it all attractive, accessible and obviously worthwhile is the key issue. Motivation – and how to encourage it – is all." (DfEE, 1999, p21)

The government's response to the Moser report was to launch the *Skills for Life Strategy,* with bold targets to increase participation and achievement in the adult population in literacy, language and numeracy by the year 2004. The targets were subsequently increased and extended to 2007. If more and different people are to be attracted into developing LLN and if the essential skills of individuals as well as UK society as a whole are to be improved, then motivation, purposes and interests must be harnessed. Embedding LLN learning could be an attractive way to draw people into learning activities while supporting them with the necessary skills that help them to achieve. This approach seems to be valid whether adults are taking tentative steps towards community-based learning, committed to full vocational programmes or entering work-based opportunities. Harnessing a personal, leisure or employment related purpose could provide the stimulus or motivation to engage in learning. Embedding the subject-related LLN could help the achievement of both the 'host' subject as well as the basic skills.

Embedding helps overcome prior failure and anxieties

For many people, the idea of returning to learning is not attractive because their initial experiences of education were unrewarding and, for some, damaging. This is particularly so in relation to LLN learning where painful memories can cloud considerations of whether to engage in taking up opportunities. A possible repetition of failure deters many adults from seeking to develop their LLN skills. An embedded approach could focus on developing an area of interest or a work-related skill where some prior knowledge and confidence might support motivation. By using such a context as a starting point and embedding LLN within the activity, negative attitudes might be addressed and positive learning experiences offered.

Embedding supports achievement of wider goals and ambitions

Embedding LLN in other subjects or learning activities is important because it helps people to achieve wider personal and employment ambitions and taps into individual purposes and motivations. Importantly, learners are not told to improve their LLN skills before moving into their chosen area of study; they can pursue their aims and aspirations immediately. In workplace learning where employees have insecure LLN skills, progress and development in the job can be more effective if LLN learning is embedded.

Embedding helps both subject and LLN teachers

The development of LLN in other courses helps teachers to deliver more effective learning. The 'host' subject tutor has more tools to help learners achieve and the LLN tutor has a clear context and purpose in which to deliver LLN learning. Where teachers make the connections explicit the host subject and LLN become mutually supportive areas of learning. Learners are then more likely to see the relevant links between the subject and the LLN and recognise the necessity to develop in both areas. In response to questions about the importance of embedded LLN, quotations from providers, practitioners and policy-makers have included:

"It's motivational!"

"It takes basic skills out of its silo."

"It's a rich way of working; it is more mainstream than discrete provision. Many people who are disaffected need an holistic approach to learning; embedded basic skills offers this."

"It's supportive; if you're on a vocational programme, it helps you to achieve your goal."

2 The origins & development of embedded literacy, language and numeracy

As already indicated, the idea of using learner motivations, purposes and contexts to stimulate and maintain interest in LLN learning has been a central part of its development and is not a new revelation. It could be claimed that the development of a distinctive and clear 'genre' of embedded LLN delivery is new. However, such a development draws on strong traditions of practice.

Core and key skills

The development of core skills alongside National Vocational Qualifications (NVQs) during the 1980s and 1990s was seen as promoting the essential skills needed to achieve a main programme of study. These skills were defined as those that are necessary to perform in a wide range of employment and life activities, some of which had previously been described as the '3Rs'. The Dearing Report (1996) suggested that they should be called key skills and the Further Education Funding Council (FEFC) strongly advocated that:

> "Wherever possible, key skills should be integrated with other aspects of the course. The degree to which this happens varies between colleges, study programmes and the different key skills." (FEFC, 1998, p20)

The purpose of teaching these skills was to help learners, not only achieve on the host programme but also to achieve the appropriate level of key skills. The vocational programme provided the context for supporting literacy, language or numeracy learning. The FEFC further suggested

> "Where key skills are integral to the course and seen to be relevant, students generally make successful progress in acquiring them." (FEFC, 1998, p20)

Key skills and LLN draw on the same standards at levels 1 and 2. (QCA, 2000)

ESOL and ESP

In drawing on the traditions of ESOL, English for Specific Purposes (ESP) and English as a Foreign Language (EFL), examples of embedding can be found. Nicholls and Naish (1981) suggested that using real situations, related to the motivations of learners would lead to effective learning. Sometimes such programmes of learning were referred to as 'linked skills'. Learners were motivated either by the relevance of the host subject or by the language content, which they developed because of the attractiveness of the context. ESP emerged as a sub-division of EFL or ESOL and included embedding English in specific commercial, professional work-related activities. This might include English for airline pilots or for textile buyers. Not only does the learning purpose or the workplace provide the 'host' subject, but some expertise can lie with the learners. They provide knowledge of the subject and the tutor offers the relevant English; a mutually supportive teaching and learning partnership can develop.

Additional support

The FEFC recognised that many individual learners could achieve on their chosen programme of study, if they were offered additional support with LLN. Its funding methodology allowed extra money to be claimed to provide such support. In reporting on the effectiveness of additional support, Green and Milbourne (1998) suggested that effective liaison between the subject tutor and the basic skills tutor was vital in planning and delivering LLN. The model of delivery suggests that individual learners were motivated to learn basic skills because they wanted to achieve their primary, vocational goal. This tradition is based on the assessment of an individual's LLN abilities compared with the LLN requirements of a particular vocational programme and not on a curriculum model of embedding LLN. It has also been suggested, many years earlier, that a vision of embedded provision should be one where the competences necessary for academic and vocational subjects should be shared between subject and basic skills staff and agreed within a common framework for delivery. There are clear lessons to be drawn from this way of delivering LLN.

Workplace learning

Where the workplace, the job or future employment is the purpose for learning, this could be described as the host subject. Case studies produced by the Basic Skills Agency and the Trades Union Congress (2000), suggested that where the LLN requirements of a job activity were analysed, a purposeful and responsive curriculum could be developed. The relevance of the curriculum, combined with the necessary LLN skills created learning that motivated employees and helped them to achieve. Rhoder and French discovered in 1994 that successful learning programmes for hospital staff were related to:

> "...their department, the hospital and their personal lives. In this way, reading and writing tasks dealt with issues and problems that were meaningful to the participants. (Rhoder and French, 1995, p112)

Those who gained from such learning were not only the individuals but also their employers and those for whom hospital services were offered. Such an approach was endorsed by the Workplace Basic Skills Training Network (2002). It suggested that training in transport, food retailing, the distribution sectors, the print, media and creative industries, hospitality, tourism and the public sector should involve negotiating programmes of learning that included LLN.

Community-based learning

Another area where an approach to embedding basic skills seems to have grown is where a host subject is planned to attract new and different learners to return to learning. This is often in community-based learning. Within such motivational, often 'first step' learning, the subject is seen as a 'hook' to attract people and convince them that learning can be fun and rewarding. Such learners are often perceived as reluctant to declare that they need or want to develop their LLN skills and so embedding is seen as a non-threatening approach. The close links between the host subject and LLN are planned from the outset. The interests, contexts, personal situations, community-focused issues, domestic or economic purposes of the individuals or groups are considered along with the LLN curricula. A learning programme is then designed taking these influences into account. On many occasions, the programme is designed with the learners and often with the close co-operation of a voluntary or community organisation. Where an organisation such as a housing charity, a drug or alcohol abuse agency, a women's refuge or a drop-in for unemployed people sees that learning can add value to their services, programmes are jointly planned and delivered.

The final report of the Voluntary and Community Sector Basic Skills and ESOL Fund (2001) suggested that many voluntary and community groups have been unwilling to see basic skills as a discrete subject. They have woven LLN into a wider picture of community action such as promoting the introduction of traffic-calming measures in Lancaster or assessing issues of employment and employ-ability in Derby (NIACE, 2001). Similarly, the Basic Skills in Local Communities report (LSC, 2004) found that many projects attracted new learners by offering LLN through another subject. The report suggested that ICT was a popular host subject.

Family learning

Family learning, including family literacy and numeracy, could be described as another approach to embedding LLN learning. Where parents and carers are attracted into learning so that they can help their children, they often learn about literacy and numeracy as well as strategies for supporting their children in these areas. While learning how to help their children, they develop their own LLN skills too. The host subject of helping a child is enhanced through the embedding of

INSPIRATIONS

The Riverside Credit Union

Local people have taken responsibility for running this Credit Union. They have also developed a scheme for families to buy baby equipment at highly competitive prices. Through volunteering and running the services, they have developed not only money management skills and related numeracy but also communication skills. Learning activities address ways of using and developing these skills and are embedded in the process of learning how to run their enterprises.

(ACLF project 2002-2004)

"Many projects, particularly those aimed at developing literacy skills, used embedded basic skills courses as the means of doing this. Learners on many of these courses were able to work towards achieving other kinds of nationally recognised qualifications. The most popular were in IT."

(LSC, 2004, p31)

Family Signing

In Northampton parents of deaf and hearing-impaired children felt that they couldn't communicate effectively with their children. The families learned to communicate with one another using not only signing but also lip-reading, reading and writing; a programme of family learning was designed to meet their specific interests and needs. Parents' communication skills developed, their language awareness increased, they were able to help their children's language development and further learning opportunities opened up for both parents and children.

(ACLF project 2002)

LLN. Both areas of learning need to draw on two areas of expertise and to be planned and reviewed together. In wider family learning where adults and children learn together through such activities as sport, creative arts, family history, music or performance, LLN has been woven into the curriculum.

Practitioners, providers and policy-makers have long realised that offering discrete LLN activities only attracts people who feel able to declare that they want assistance with these essential skills. They have, over many years, experimented with ways of linking or embedding LLN with vocational, academic or personal learning activities.

Richard Olivier

3 Defining embedded literacy, language and numeracy

"Embedded teaching and learning combines the development of literacy, language and numeracy with vocational and other skills. The skills acquired provide learners with the confidence, competence and motivation necessary for them to succeed in qualifications, in life and at work. (DfES/The National Research and Development Centre (NRDC))" (DfES, 2004, p6)

This is probably the most recent definition of what is meant by embedded LLN and is a helpful summary of a complex and multi-facted approach to teaching and learning.

A NIACE research project in 2002-3 developed a working definition which was changed and refined over the period of the research (NIACE, 2003, unpublished). It attempted to capture what practitioners, providers and policy makers, involved in the research, suggested embedded LLN should be. The following definition is based on that work.

Embedded literacy, language and numeracy is an approach to teaching those skill areas within another learning programme. The embedding occurs throughout the whole strategy for delivering the course, including recruitment, assessment, staffing and learning materials. Although the delivery of LLN is embedded, it is explicit. Learners know their course will help them with their LLN; they have learning outcomes that focus on LLN as well as the host subject and achievement is identified in both areas of learning. Learners can be offered accreditation in both the host subject and in LLN. Teaching LLN in an embedded way usually involves using materials, which exploit the learners' interests, involvement and requirements of the host subject whilst developing their LLN skills.

The key features of this definition are that:

- The learners know that LLN learning is part of their learning activity;
- Learning outcomes are identified in both the host subject and in LLN;
- The concept of embedding LLN is applied at all stages of planning, delivering and identifying achievement.

There appears to be an occasional interchange of the terms embedded LLN and contextualised LLN. It is possible to suggest that they draw on similar origins and development but that they emerge as two distinct approaches to teaching and learning. Contextualised LLN learning is where the primary learning goal is one associated with LLN and where tutors draw into their teaching and learning programmes, contexts, topics and issues which are relevant to the identified interests, purposes and needs of individuals or groups. Embedded learning is where the host subject is the primary or equal learning goal along with LLN but where the LLN is identified, taught and learned within the host subject and supports achievement of it.

Linked learning or integrated learning have also been used to describe teaching and learning approaches to delivering LLN with a host subject. They appear to refer to very similar approaches to embedded learning. For the purposes of this publication, the term 'embedded' has been adopted.

Richard Olivier

4 The challenges

While embedding appears to be a sensible approach to developing adult LLN skills, the reality is that it is an extremely challenging area of development. Many questions remain unanswered or partially answered and ongoing research can help to address them (The National Research and Development Centre for Adult Literacy and Numeracy is involved in such research). Some of the challenges include:

- Does a whole organisation approach to embedding need to be in place?
- What infrastructures support a whole organisation approach?
- When should learners be told about the LLN content of their programme? How do we ensure they are not 'put off' but are informed?
- How and when should screening, initial and diagnostic assessment be carried out?
- What does an Individual Learning Plan look like, where two areas of learning are being addressed?
- What staff skills are needed?
- How many staff are needed?
- How do staff ensure that both areas of learning receive an appropriate level of attention?
- What makes embedded LLN work?
- How is progress and achievement recognised and recorded in two areas of learning?
- How are learners supported to progress? What kinds of progression routes should be offered?
- What would inspectors look for?
- How is embedded LLN funded?

Some of these questions are addressed in this Lifeline; others are subject to further research and development.

5 Models of delivery

The NIACE research worked with practitioner-researchers to try to identify and describe the models of delivery that were offered as embedded approaches. All the practitioner-researchers believed that they were involved in delivering some form of embedded LLN. The research enabled them to develop, reflect and refine their approaches. While there are no prescribed models it is helpful to examine those which seem to reflect the majority of approaches.

Model 1 – fully embedded

This model, which appears especially at pre-entry level of delivery, can be described as a fully embedded model. It is usually a short or part-time programme, delivered by one tutor who is trained in the delivery of LLN but who also has host subject knowledge. In this model, the LLN is woven throughout the delivery of the programme and there is usually one learning aim that is associated with the host subject. However, other individual learning outcomes are usually identified which are associated with LLN.

Cambridge Regional College

Cambridge Regional College delivered a short customer-care course to carers working in the NHS. Careful assessment of their work environment, requirements of their work and the challenges they identified in day-to-day working informed the design of the 21-hour programme. The tutor identified the skills they needed to develop their roles and mapped them to the literacy standards. As the majority of the carers work related directly to the literacy core curriculum, it was relatively easy to deliver the customer-care course outcomes through an embedded approach. Learners felt they had developed their customer care skills as well as reading, writing, speaking and listening.
(DEBS project 2002-3)

Model 2 – a sandwich model

This delivery model is based on a 50%–50% approach between the host subject and LLN; all the LLN content is based on the requirements of the host subject. Some models are quite strictly divided between the two areas of development while, more commonly, the divisions are flexible from session to session while retaining an overall 50%–50% split. In some instances, the availability of practical resources dictates how much time is spent on LLN with, for example, half a session spent on the host, practical activities and the other half spent on the associated LLN. This model is found in part-time courses but delivered in different ways. Some organisations use one teacher who has support from a LLN expert while others use two teachers who work as a team. Some models use one teacher who has both host subject and LLN teaching skills and experience. Where two staff work closely together with both of them becoming aware of the needs of the learners in relation to the programme of study and the LLN requirements, effective embedding takes place. The spin-offs of a team-teaching approach are associated with sharing specialist knowledge as well as different teaching and learning styles and methods.

INSPIRATIONS

Everyday Money Management

Northamptonshire Lifelong Learning Service delivered a short, part-time course in relation to Everyday Money Management. While the course aimed to develop money management skills it also aimed to develop knowledge about debt, financial services, banks, and credit unions. Within this subject, individuals were able to indicate what basic numeracy skills they needed to work on. These skills were developed alongside the broader social and economic issues surrounding financial management.
(DEBS project 2002-3)

Model 3 – overlapping circles of study

This model emerges as relevant to both short- and long-term courses. The balance between the subject and the LLN varies from session to session according to the content and the needs of the learners. Typically, programmes start with some periods of time for the vocational/host subject to be delivered completely separately from the LLN content. Very quickly these two areas overlap and it is here that the embedding of the LLN appears to take place.

Overlapping circles model

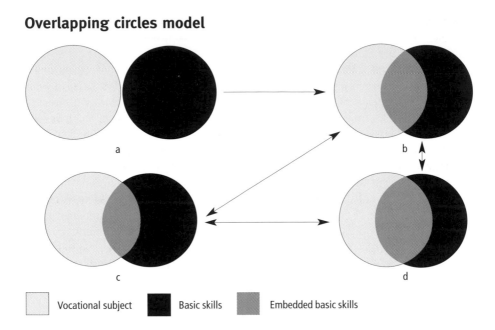

| | Vocational subject | | Basic skills | | Embedded basic skills |

As with model 2, staff delivery varies between one teacher with specialist knowledge in both curriculum areas on short courses to two teachers team teaching, one teacher being supported by a LLN specialist or one teacher supported by a trained volunteer on longer courses.

INSPIRATIONS

Rodbaston College

Rodbaston College delivers LLN embedded in Animal Care, Horticulture, Agriculture, Equine Studies and Countryside Management courses. These programmes run for 24 hours per week and students are taught three hours per week by LLN specialist staff who ensure vocational relevance in their materials. Vocational staff also teach LLN within their sessions and make LLN skills explicit in their planning. A team approach to planning is adopted so that an embedded approach is an assumed and automatic process.

(DEBS project 2002-3)

These models are indicative and not prescriptive. There are some features which should be present in all models:

- learners' purposes and motivations should be paramount;
- programmes and organisations should develop their own approaches, which may be variations of the above;
- all models should be designed to deliver both a host subject and LLN, with learning outcomes identified in both areas;
- the model of delivery will be influenced by the host subject, organisational structures, staff skills and experience and availability of resources;
- each curriculum area can influence the other;
- two areas of expertise must be acknowledged; these can be delivered by one person or through a team approach.

There is however, a health warning. By focusing on a delivery model the purpose of embedding LLN may be lost. What is important is that the needs of learners and potential learners are considered in relation to both the host subject and the LLN content and the embedded programme designed around those. The purposes of embedding LLN must be carefully considered.

Sue Parkins, NIACE

6 Planning for delivery

Whole organisational approach

Embedding LLN in learning programmes across a whole organisation ensures consistency, coherence and a commitment to a learning entitlement. If a whole organisation realises the benefits of embedding LLN, in all programmes up to and including level 2, for example, learners will have many choices for progression open to them. They will also be assured of the necessary support to develop their literacy, language and numeracy with the skills and knowledge required for the subject or work activity of their choice. This is an ambitious but not unrealistic aim.

Colleges

In colleges, senior managers should create plans to embed LLN which are systematically operationalised and supported by relevant staff training and development. Working links should be supported and encouraged between LLN staff and vocational and academic staff. Time must be committed to building relationships, trust and understanding of each other's curriculum area. On such foundations, learners can pursue their interests and aspirations, knowing that the necessary LLN content of any programme of learning is addressed and not left to chance. Participation in LLN learning can be 'normalised' as everyone gets involved. Staff can encourage progression along a range of routes, confident that LLN tuition will be automatically available to support achievement. This approach does not necessarily negate the need for individual additional learning support but it should reduce and more precisely focus the use of it. The embedded curriculum should ensure more learners achieve in their host subject as well as improve their LLN skills.

Community-based learning

In community-based learning, organisations should adopt similar strategic approaches. Strong relationships should be developed between subject and LLN specialist staff. All programmes can be reviewed for their LLN content and the skills identified which support the achievement of the host subject.

Workplace

Similarly, in the workplace, strategic planning can ensure that whatever work-related development is planned, the essential LLN skills are identified which support achievement of the activities. Designing workplace learning should include development of the associated LLN skills. This means drawing on both areas of expertise either through one coach, trainer or teacher or through team teaching.

All organisations concerned with teaching and learning should include statements about embedding LLN in their strategic and operational plans.

Successful planning

Planning at both a strategic and operational level is not simple. However, there are some essential features, which can lead to successful delivery. They seem to focus on time and skills:

- Two areas of expertise should be involved: the host subject and LLN.
- Time should be committed where staff need to work in partnership in order to embed LLN in a host subject. Such partnerships can involve team teaching; the LLN expert can act as a consultant to the subject tutor.
- Where a partnership is with an external organisation or agency, time must be dedicated to building trust and understanding as well as curriculum development.
- Infra-structure materials such as initial and diagnostic assessment activities, schemes of work, lesson plans and individual learning plans should be adopted or designed, which support the development of the entwined strands of learning.
- Materials and resources should be identified or made which meet the requirements of both strands of activity.
- Extra time may be needed where dual accreditation is involved.
- Staff training may be needed to build capacity about LLN within vocational and academic staff teams.
- Similarly, training and development may be needed to build capacity about host subject areas within LLN staff teams.
- Mapping host subject curricula to the LLN standards is needed but mapping alone does not lead to an embedded approach. Mapping identifies the possible opportunities to develop LLN but teachers should decide what, how and when these opportunities are exploited.
- Consideration must be given to the design of the Individual Learning Plan (where one is used), so that activities and achievements in both the host subject and LLN are recognised and recorded.
- Tutorial time should be built into programme designs so that individual review and reflection can take place; this ensures that learners are clear about their learning achievements as well as the next goals and steps they should take.

Qualified staff

Teachers of both curriculum areas should be appropriately qualified. Subject tutors should have knowledge, experience and qualifications in their subject area as well as a nationally recognised teaching qualification. LLN tutors should also have the necessary level of knowledge of their specialist subject as well as an appropriate teaching qualification. Vocational staff could obtain additional LLN teaching qualifications to enhance the delivery of their subjects. Details of the qualifications required for staff to perform different roles in adult literacy, language and numeracy teaching and learning are available on the Qualifications and Curriculum Authority website: www.qca.org.uk

Where there is commitment to embed LLN across a whole organisation, the use of a 'champion' could be considered. This would be an individual to whom others could turn for support, information and advice but their very presence would demonstrate a serious commitment to the embedded LLN approach.

Rodbaston College

Rodbaston College has developed a whole organisation approach to delivering embedded LLN and offered financial incentives to all staff who complete specialist LLN qualifications. The management has made a clear commitment to staff and students to help in achieving the organisational aims; the outcome ensures coherence across the whole college.
(DEBS project 2002-3)

Champion for embedding LLN

Increasing numbers of general colleges of further education give a member of the senior management team responsibility for LLN within the organisation. This person helps to advocate and support the specialist role for LLN, encouraging all departments and programmes to engage with the curriculum. The approach helps to break down departmental divisions and embed LLN across the whole organisation.

7 Promoting embedded literacy, language and numeracy

Different audiences are addressed when trying to promote embedded LLN learning opportunities. Some people are reluctant learners and feel that learning is not for them. Others are keen to learn but may be anxious that their LLN skills are not 'up to speed', whilst some may be keen to learn and unaware that their LLN skills may pose a barrier to success. Embedding learning can offer something to all these groups but promotion and publicity materials need to take account of their different attitudes and feelings.

Where learners are keen to pursue an interest or a vocational programme or develop skills at work, offering embedded LLN can be a bonus. Publicity materials should emphasise the additional features available in a positive manner. Where learners may be deterred from pursuing their interests and ambitions due to their anxieties about their LLN skills, promotion should be reassuring, offering LLN tuition as part of a supportive programme. In those programmes which are designed to encourage and 'hook' people back into learning, the sensitivities around publicity become more problematic. The question is, when are learners encouraged by knowing that LLN tuition is included and when are they deterred?

When the adults involved require ESOL tuition, such sensitivities are usually irrelevant. The majority, although not all, ESOL learners are keen to pursue learning and providers often report waiting lists. In such situations, ESOL learners see embedded provision as offering a double bargain; they get language tuition along side other activities such as ICT, practical subjects or employment-related learning.

Some providers are reluctant to mention LLN in their publicity materials in case learners are deterred and prefer to talk about this at a later stage in the process. For some individuals this can be helpful; they have a chance to get to know someone before confronting their anxieties. For others however, this approach can be seen as deceitful and are further put off returning to learning.

Yet again, placing the potential learners at the heart of consideration and empathising with their situation seems to be the key to success in influencing the design of the promotion and publicity. Clear information about what is on offer should be available, with an emphasis on what might attract and interest the learners. However, the LLN content should be evident, particularly demonstrating its relevance to the achievement of the host subject. Using such terms as 'communication skills' and 'using maths', in association with the subject seems to work.

The following example shows how naturally LLN content can be included in publicity material.

Havering College

Havering College promoted an aromatherapy course using a simple format:

Aromatherapy Massage

Free 10 week course

Come and learn about:
- **what aromatherapy is;**
- **how to give hand, foot, neck and shoulder massage;**
- **the refreshing and uplifting (as well as calming and relaxing) benefits of aromatherapy essential oils;**
- **how to make an aromatherapy blend;**
- **the healing benefits of massage;**
- **how to be confident in communication skills.**

Starting soon at the Wykeham Centre.

Limited places available so please visit or call the centre on...

As in most activities designed to attract new learners, the most effective strategies are those which include face-to-face work. Outreach with agencies and organisations which might host learning events and activities can tap into people with whom they are in regular contact. This can include health centres, primary schools, hostels for homeless people, women's centres, faith centres and community halls. Such agencies can act as 'signposts' to encourage and support new learners. They can also help tutors understand the needs and motivations of the groups with whom they work.

Holding market stalls and joining other promotional events, such as fairs and festivals can be productive because people are present to explain, reassure and offer additional information. However, in all these activities, some written information is usually needed so that people can take them away, along with contact details. Using the Basic Skills Agency (BSA) SMOG test can help in designing publicity at the best language level for the target group.

The West Cumbria WEA

The West Cumbria WEA developed literacy and numeracy through music and songwriting. They suggested:

"You might like to get your learners to produce eye-catching posters to promote their group."

This approach means that new learners receive the insights gained by existing learners about what the course/programme can do/has done for them. (ACLF project 2002-4)

Richard Olivier

8 Screening, initial assessment and diagnostic assessment

What are they?

- *Screening* tools are used to find out whether or not someone might have a literacy, language or numeracy need.
- *Initial assessment* will help identify learners' skills against a level or levels within the national standards. Learners may have different levels of reading, writing, numeracy and language skills. Initial assessment is often used to help place learners in appropriate learning programmes. It is usually followed by detailed diagnostic assessment.
- *Diagnostic assessment* is designed to provide a detailed assessment of a learner's skills and abilities against the requirements set out in the national standards. The assessment results can be used as the basis for the learner's individual learning plan and the learning programme.

Readwriteplus website: www.dfes.gov.uk/readwriteplus/teachingandlearning

Where embedding LLN takes place within a college or work-based setting on a full-time programme there are usually established expectations that all new learners are screened for LLN abilities at the beginning of their programmes. This means that any anxieties surrounding LLN can be identified, hopefully in a supportive and positive manner, but also as a matter of course. Such an approach can help learners feel that they are not being 'exposed' when such procedures are the norm for all learners. Where areas for LLN development are identified through screening, there are usually systems in place to conduct follow-up initial assessment activities. Diagnostic assessment follows initial assessment. Sometimes, diagnostic assessment is completed as part of an on-going assessment process and the differences are not sharply made. On full-time and substantial part-time programmes it seems sensible to gradually work towards assessing what learners can and cannot do, in relation to LLN, so that responsive and realisable learning plans can be drafted. This does not necessarily mean that one 'test' or assessment should follow another. Good assessment practices use a range of activities, over a period of time, negotiated with the learner to determine where the emphasis of a learning plan should lie. In substantial programmes it is easier to incorporate such practices using a mixture of home-grown and commercially published assessment materials. Published materials for initial assessment can include such things as:

- BSA Initial Assessment;
- Target Skills;
- Key Skills Builder;

as well as learners' writing, reading, self-assessment, proof-reading and correction activities. The BSA Diagnostic Assessment Pack can assist in the next stages of assessing what learners can already do and what they need to work on. However, it is vital that the learner is involved in the process and talking about past and current practices and activities can reveal a great deal of insight.

Screening, initial assessment and diagnostic assessment become more challenging in short programmes, especially where they are designed to attract reluctant learners into provision. Similar challenges arise in workplace settings where learning activities are often short and very specific. Some kind of initial, informal screening process should be used so that organisers are sure that they are attracting the least well-qualified learners. If publicity and promotion activities lead to attracting people to host subjects who do not need to develop LLN, signposting to other provision must take place. Screening activities can include careful and sensitive questioning and discussion at an initial interview, the completion of 'can do' lists or such broad indicators as achievement of grade C or below in GCSEs in English or Maths. Such approaches can be usually used without fear of deterring new learners. Some short community programmes are planned so that their whole purpose is one of assessment. They are designed to gradually encourage learners to see for themselves where their LLN strengths lie and what they could develop.

At the end of such short programmes the evidence of the learners' interests and abilities in both the host subject and LLN should be clearer to the learner and the tutor. Information and advice can be offered to learners, based around what has been revealed and developed. Guidance to more discrete LLN learning opportunities, further embedded opportunities or host subject courses could result.

In embedded LLN courses, the relevance of the initial assessment and diagnostic assessment processes are of paramount importance. Using materials, which are based on the host subject and related to activities in the learning programme, can be subtle ways of assessing learners' abilities in LLN. For example, using an introductory writing frame to identify what learners already know, want to gain from a course and hope to achieve can reveal many indicators about text, sentence and word level literacy activities. Using discussions, small groups and individual presentations can indicate speaking and listening skills. Learning activities and tasks can be planned over a number of sessions so that they gradually reveal what learners can do. On the Northampton Lifelong Learning Money Management programme, tutors were able to track numeracy skills through tasks related to the programme. Learners revealed what they could do and tutors recorded that on tracking sheets. These sheets were later used to inform the ILP.

INSPIRATIONS

The recently published *Planning learning and recording progress and achievement: a guide for practitioners* explains how,

"Assessment takes many different forms and is used for a range of purposes."

The guide explains these different forms of assessment in three layers of detail.
(DfES, 2004, p9)

Approaches to Assessment

The WEA in West Cumbria acknowledged the jargon used in learning and its potential to discourage learners.

"Assessment is not a term that learners use or like to use. The word has overtones of being judgemental. However, all learners love feedback. They like to receive lots of feedback, so tutors should be aware of the importance of giving feedback, using their skills in: listening, observing, checking learning progress, encouraging reflective practice, giving one to one feedback and assessing what the next step for each learner could be."
(ACLF final report 2004)

Careful thought and planning should be committed to screening, initial and diagnostic assessment in the context of the purposes of the learning activity. The processes must be 'fit for purpose', sensitive to the new learners and their situation and designed to learn as much as possible about what they can and cannot do. Recording such information, as simply and as efficiently as possible, is important so that the subsequent ILP and programme is responsive. There is no single initial or diagnostic assessment tool suitable for all contexts or all target groups.

9 Individual learning plans

One of the dilemmas for providers of embedded LLN is to decide whether to produce one or two Individual Learning Plans (ILPs). One ILP must include aims for both the host subject and the LLN content; two ILPs for the separate strands must be linked and shared between staff. The response to this dilemma is to ask which approach best serves the interest of the learners; there is no one answer.

ILPs record the learning aims of a programme or activity. A learning aim may be an accreditation or a qualification. It may be a statement of what a particular course sets out to do and achieve; this is a non-accredited learning aim. As already indicated, in embedded LLN models of delivery there may be a single learning aim, supported by a range of learning outcomes which reflect the host subject and LLN. There may be two learning aims, drawn from the two curriculum areas.

Some programmes produce a common ILP for a group, which captures the main programme aim and anticipated learning outcomes but with space for the addition of personal learning goals.

INSPIRATIONS

Individual Learning Plans (ILP)

Tower Hamlets College has piloted a model of an ILP which records the programme aim and the planned outcomes. Learners then add their own anticipated goals, following involvement in the course. The plan records pre-printed curriculum outcomes, linked to the literacy, language or numeracy core curricula and is used to capture what learners can do and where they need further work and practice. It also has space to record the outcomes of tutorial reviews.
(DEBS project 2002-3)

The importance of ILPs is that learners can determine what they are working towards and indicate their longer term goals in relation to the learning programme. The language they use to describe these goals must relate to what they want to do; goals, which are described by a tutor in relation to curricula outcomes do not generally use the language of learners. It is important that goals are expressed in learners' own language. This is particularly challenging where some ESOL learners are concerned or where the learners have learning difficulties and/or disabilities. Sometimes a group of learners will determine what goals they want to pursue. These should be recorded and shared with all members of the group and the staff team.

Goals must be SMART. This means that they are:

Specific	Focussed and clear;
Measurable	Learners and tutors will know what evidence to look for;
Achievable	Manageable enough to complete successfully with the resources available and within the learners' ability range;
Relevant and	Matched to the purposes and motivations of the learner;
Timebound	Can be completed in the time allocated.

Goal setting

The kind of goals a learner might record on an embedded LLN and Beauty course:

By the end of next term I will be able to:

- speak to customers in the salon;
- accurately record the dye mixtures used;
- accurately keep the appointments diary up to date;
- staff the salon reception desk on my own.

Goals should be reviewed regularly, not only with the learners and tutors but also within the adult staff team. This requires a planning assumption that tutorial time is available for learners and review time is available for staff teams.

The steps which individuals take towards achieving their goals are known as targets. These are much smaller than goals and are the 'building blocks' of which goals are made. In working towards the wider goals outlined above for a beauty programme, targets would include activities related to speaking with individuals who are known to the learner as well as strangers. Such activities would be carried out on several occasions, in different situations such as at reception, in the waiting area, during treatments and might be observed, tape or video recorded with opportunities for feedback and review. These targets would be, like the goals, SMART.

Goals and targets can be negotiated which are about more general things than skills or knowledge. Some learners will speak of wanting to feel more confident in particular situations or with particular activities. These are perfectly legitimate goals and targets, activities should be planned to offer learning opportunities to achieve them. Evidence of progress towards achievement should be gathered so that the learner can see that gains are being made.

The above example indicates how in an embedded model of delivery the host subject, beauty, is clearly being worked on but the literacy and language skills of speaking and listening are also being addressed.

The *Planning Learning and Recording Progress and Achievement: a Guide for practitioners* (DfES, 2004) publication provides detailed insight into developing and using ILPs.

Richard Olivier

10 Delivering embedded literacy, language and numeracy

Providers and practitioners have used a wide range of subjects and situations in which to embed LLN delivery. They include:

Learning activity	Organisation
Sport	A housing association
Vehicle Maintenance	A Council for Voluntary Service
Cooking on a budget	A Sure Start programme
Local history	LEA Adult Education Service
Photography	Homelessness organisation
Tourism	College of Further Education
Catering	College of Further Education
Work Skills and ESOL	College of Further Education
Adult Rural Skills	Agricultural College
Hairdressing	College of Further Education
Living skills	Voluntary and Community provider (WEA)

The list, taken from the Developing Embedded Basic Skills (DEBS) work (2002-3), indicates that embedding LLN can take place in any subject and with any provider.
A clear process pre-supposes the delivery of embedded LLN:

Planning delivery of embedded LLN

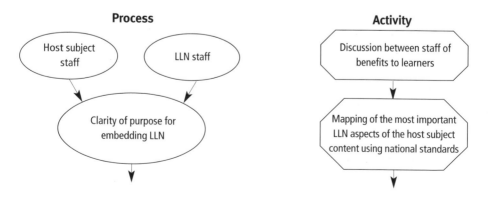

Process

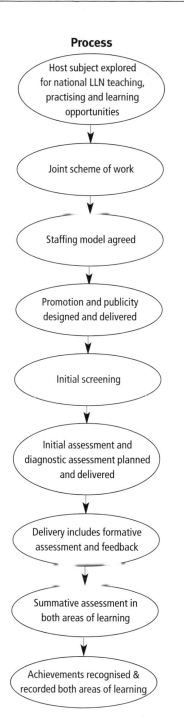

Host subject explored for national LLN teaching, practising and learning opportunities

Joint scheme of work

Staffing model agreed

Promotion and publicity designed and delivered

Initial screening

Initial assessment and diagnostic assessment planned and delivered

Delivery includes formative assessment and feedback

Summative assessment in both areas of learning

Achievements recognised & recorded both areas of learning

Activity

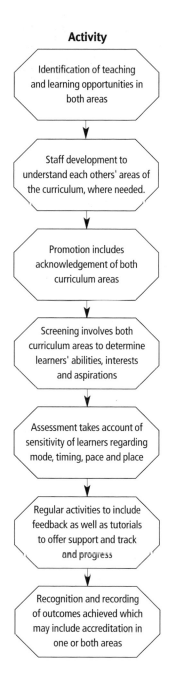

Identification of teaching and learning opportunities in both areas

Staff development to understand each others' areas of the curriculum, where needed.

Promotion includes acknowledgement of both curriculum areas

Screening involves both curriculum areas to determine learners' abilities, interests and aspirations

Assessment takes account of sensitivity of learners regarding mode, timing, pace and place

Regular activities to include feedback as well as tutorials to offer support and track and progress

Recognition and recording of outcomes achieved which may include accreditation in one or both areas

Once the preparation steps are completed, session plans and tutorial time can be designed which take account of the learners' ability profiles, interests and motivations as well as the curriculum demands of the host subject and the embedded LLN. There is a danger associated with attempting to embed LLN throughout all aspects of the host subject; it might result in a paper exercise that is meaningless for learners and tutors. Where courses link the LLN content to the subject and consider the impact this will have on the individual learners, the group and the overall course, the most effective results seem to emerge. Mapping of LLN against the National Occupational Standards for over 170 National Vocational Qualifications (NVQs) is available on the DfES website.

Scheme of work

Schemes of work offer the framework for a programme of learning. In embedding LLN, the scheme of work should indicate that both LLN and the host subject will be taught and assessed. Havering College designed a scheme of work, which recorded learning outcomes for both curriculum areas; the scheme informed the development of session plans:

The Learning Freeway Aromatherapy Massage course used these headings to frame the scheme of work:

Week	Core curriculum content	Learner activities	Learner outcomes	Assessment/ evidence	Teaching methods
2	Speaking and listening (ref to core curriculum)	What is aromatherapy?	Learner shows listening and demonstrates understanding	Question and answer quiz	Exposition Discussion Individual and group work

Lesson plans

Rodbaston College designed lesson plans that included headings concerning activity and content, the key or basic skills being developed and the resources needed as well as the usual indications of date, lesson duration, topic and objective. In addition, questions were posed which asked how staff would differentiate and any special points to note regarding student abilities. The following is an adaptation of their plan:

Lesson content and activities	Topic Employment in the fishing industry	Objective The students will be able to…
How are you going to differentiate?	Date	Venue
Special points to note?		
Activity and content	Key/basic skills (ref core curriculum)	Resources
9.45am… 10.15am… 10.45am Break 11.00am… 11.30am… 12.00pm Round up		
Next session: Reminder to bring:		
Forward planning		Lesson evaluation See checklist

The lesson plan included LLN within the topic of the fishing industry.

Course reviews

During the delivery phase, the staff team should regularly review progress of the whole course or programme. This builds close working relationships and encourages understanding of where challenges may arise and opportunities created. For example, where a subject tutor uses an item of 'real' material, different expectations can be raised when an LLN tutor uses the same material. The purposes of using the material are often different and where embedded approaches are used, such differences should be addressed. Learners should be aware that one learning activity can result in several outcomes. Similarly, one activity can be assessed for the purposes of both the host subject and LLN. There are distinct advantages for learners when such a joint approach is used. It demonstrates the close links between LLN and the host subject. Reviews help to ensure that both aspects of the programme are addressed.

Additional learning support

Additional learning support should, wherever possible, be accessed for learners. This would include such things as support with sensory and physical disabilities, dyslexia and in some cases, additional literacy, language or numeracy, according to the screening and assessment information.

Tutorial support

Tutorial support has been identified as making a particularly important contribution to embedded LLN approaches. This is so, regardless of the setting or the duration of the programme. On longer courses, more tutorials should be planned. Tutorial time offers the opportunity to review learning with groups and individuals, the identification of challenges as well as of progress and achievements. Negotiating new goals and targets can take place during tutorial time, in the light of feedback and review. Records of tutorials should be kept which indicate the issues discussed as well as the actions agreed. ILPs are the best places to record progress, comments or concerns in both the host subject and LLN.

Tutorials

"Having easy access to a personal tutor and guidance was an important feature of many projects. They provided structured tutorial support as well as informal support outside sessions and between sessions.."

(LSC, 2004, p19)

Materials

Materials, appropriate to the subject and the LLN objectives can be difficult to find; many projects design their own or adapt real or environmental materials for particular purposes. The latter approach is probably one that is most effective but can be time consuming; it demands that both tutors work together to identify good quality, accuracy, how the materials can be used and what outcomes can be expected. Patchwork Housing Association used sports activities and materials to embed LLN. They used rules and instructions as well as time and fitness measurements for development of LLN. Online materials and resources can enhance investigation and project-based learning activities. Craven College set tasks or assignments on tourism, which demanded library research, visits, collection of information and publicity leaflets, the design of maps and gathering of internet data. The assignments clearly indicated that key and basic skills would be addressed and assessed in accessing and using such real materials and resources.

A research and development project is currently being funded by the Adult Basic Skills Strategy Unit (ABSSU) to develop materials specifically designed to develop the LLN content of vocational subjects (visit the ReadWritePlus website, cited at the back of this publication).

Joint tasks or assignments

Where assignments integrate activities in both the subject and LLN, assessment criteria should include both LLN and the subject. Assessment feedback should include suggestions for how to improve LLN and the subject; both have equal importance. In team teaching situations, two staff can conduct assessment of one task or assignment. This approach helps learners to see the vital nature of LLN to the host subject and removes the necessity to complete several assignments or activites, when one is sufficient.

11 Progress, achievement and qualifications

The delivery of embedded LLN is closely linked to the identification of progress and achievement in the host subject. The ultimate purpose of embedding LLN is to improve achievement in the host subject, whilst, at the same time, improving LLN skills, knowledge and understanding.

The Common Inspection Framework (CIF) should inform and support the development of embedded LLN in the same way that it does for all other areas of adult learning. Success in LLN is judged by whether learners:

- make progress in line with the national standards and core curriculum;
- have access to a variety of assessment techniques;
- have SMART learning goals and targets;
- are regularly assessed against the goals and targets in their ILP;
- experience accurate screening and assessment;
- have prior skills, knowledge and experience acknowledged ;
- are involved in negotiations arising from formative assessment;
- receive clear feedback of their progress which is recorded;
- gather different and relevant forms of evidence of achievement;
- keep records which describe specific learning gains;
- use outcomes from assessment to inform next stages of planning;
- have opportunities to work towards national qualifications;
- produce evidence of completing qualifications in line with regulations;
- are clear about when and how to feedback to others the progress they make.

(Adapted from *Success in Adult Literacy, Numeracy and ESOL Provision: A guide to support the Common Inspection Framework*, DfES 2002)

The key infrastructure features that support success in embedded LLN approaches are:

- screening, initial and diagnostic assessment;
- ILPs;
- reviews and tutorials;
- records.

Progress

Progress can be described as the identification of the learning gains that take a group or individual part of the way towards achieving their goals or targets

Where SMART learning goals and targets have been set, following screening and assessment, it is relatively easy to identify where learning gains have been made. Where they are vague or irrelevant to the learner or the learning activity they are difficult to identify. The ILP can form a record of work but completed activities are not evidence of progress or achievement. Progress should be assessed against the targets being worked on. Tutors should create opportunities for groups and individuals to check whether work is being undertaken which helps the targets to be achieved. These are referred to as formative reviews. Opportunities should also be created to identify and gather the evidence that demonstrates that progress is being made. Work folders, computer records, audio and video tapes can hold such evidence. In embedded provision, evidence of accurately cutting fabric, creating a piece of craft, preparing a dish, grooming a dog, painting a door or washing hair could also be included as evidence. Reviewing and reflecting on such records can help learners to see where they are making progress and build their confidence in their own abilities.

When such reflections identify progress, this should be recorded in the ILP. Some organisations use progress sheets or records that capture what learners have achieved and what they want to work on next.

In embedded LLN, the evidence of progress is often taken from the host subject activities. This evidence should allow for the identification of progress in both the host and LLN content. Such evidence would cover progress in the LLN content, which has supported success in the host subject. For example, if a learner can now lay a row of bricks accurately, the progress in the associated calculation and measurement should be included.

Group as well as individual reviews can help to identify where learning and progress is taking place. Peer review can be a supportive, affirmative and encouraging process, where learners indicate from both work evidence and observation of each other that progress is being made. Records of such activities should be kept.

As with all reviews, time should be allocated to carry them out. On longer programmes, this is easier to plan and some organisations hold review or assessment weeks. On short programmes, it may be easier to build reviews into each session so that learners become accustomed to the reflective process. Such review time can be for the whole group or, occasionally, dedicated to individual reviews. The host subject and LLN should be included.

Achievement

Achievement can be described as the acknowledgement of evidence that a learning target or goal has been fulfilled. Achievements can also be described as

INSPIRATIONS

North East Somerset Arts Creative Links

North East Somerset Arts Creative Links project developed a wide range of opportunities for different groups of people who had experienced mental ill health. One group combined writing with photography. Participants brought items of sentimental significance to create a reminiscence opportunity as the starting point. The results were collated to create booklets of their work.

(ACLF Project report 2004)

Big Issue

Big Issue vendors were encouraged to use photography to develop their literacy and numeracy skills. Costings, fractions, decimals and time along with speaking and listening, writing narrative, planning, drafting and editing photographic reviews were clear LLN skills which the proramme could develop. However, the tutor commented that:

"Using photography to teach basic skills works well, due to it being one of our most accessible visual mediums. It encourages teamwork and group discussion, and helps to build up confidence through developing a voice and achieving set goals."

(BSA, 2003, p67)

successful learning outcomes. Occasionally achievements can be identified which were not planned; often these include such things as increases in confidence, improved speaking and listening and group or relationship building. Even though they were unplanned, they should be recorded; they are important outcomes of involvement in a learning activity. These additional outcomes can be apparent in embedded LLN programmes as the two areas of study provide opportunities for creativity and development.

At the end of a learning activity whether it is a short, motivational course or a long programme, final or summative reviews should be held. On short courses, groups can reflect together on the whole learning process as well as identify what has been gained, compared with learning goals and targets set at the beginning. On longer courses, it is easier to arrange summative reviews for each learner.

Evidence of achievement can include the following:

- summative assessment activities such as set tasks, computer-based assignments, quizzes or national tests;
- written work gathered throughout the learning programme and assembled in a portfolio or booklet;
- audio and video recordings;
- photographs of activities or work in progress;
- artefacts;
- testimonies from observations in and outside the learning environment;
- learners' own reflections and stories about their use of new skills and knowledge in and outside the learning environment.

Where programmes are not designed with accreditation or qualifications in mind, but where national LLN standards have been used, achievements will be based on those standards. Learners need to know that such measurements have been used. It is important that both the host subject and the LLN achievements are identified.

Internal moderation and verification should be conducted even where external accreditation or qualifications are not part of the learning aim. This applies to both strands of activity in embedded LLN.

For externally accredited learning, the awarding body's requirements must be met in relation to evidence of achievement of learning goals, moderation and verification. Learners should be informed early in their programme about accredited opportunities, including national qualifications. Some learners will be keen to take up accreditation whilst others will be reluctant; the offer of choice is most important.

In embedded LLN, accredited achievement may relate only to the host subject. Where this is the case, learners should also be supported to identify LLN achievements, as outlined above, so that full recognition all of the learning gains can be made. In some cases, the LLN achievements may lead to further study in order to gain accreditation or qualifications. Such gains must be recorded so that the learner can transport them and be encouraged to pursue further learning opportunities. In other cases, both the subject and the LLN achievements will be accredited.

Moving on

As part of the summative review, learners should be supported to consider their next learning steps. However, information about possible routes should be made available much earlier in the learning activity. Through ongoing dialogue about the interests and aspirations of learners, next steps can be identified. Learning providers should consider what possible progression routes are available within their own organisation, through other providers in the area and through such routes as online learning. In embedded LLN learning, the routes available can include:

- further embedded LLN programmes;
- discrete LLN programmes;
- vocational or personal development/interest programmes;
- paid or voluntary work.

Learning journeys rarely take a straight route. Learners take steps in different directions towards longer-term goals and ambitions. Importantly, tutors must create time to share information and offer advice and, where necessary, bring in colleagues who are qualified in providing Information, Advice and Guidance (IAG). Where one person is involved in delivering an embedded programme it may be necessary to consult with either a subject or LLN specialist about possible progression routes.

Where learners have been involved in embedded LLN they can be motivated to take up discrete LLN activities, which lead to national qualifications. The Move On programme offers support to prepare for such qualifications and can be helpful in not only recognising achievement but also encouraging next steps.

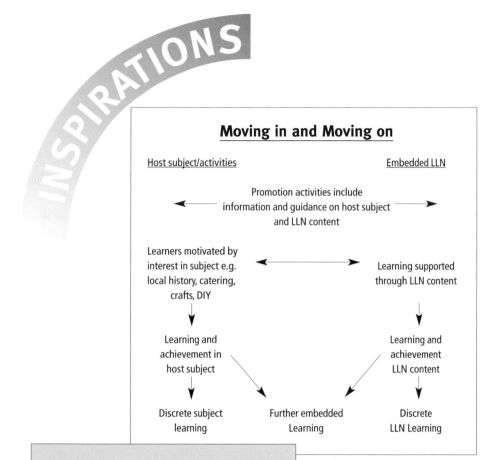

Moving in and Moving on

Host subject/activities   Embedded LLN

Promotion activities include
information and guidance on host subject
and LLN content

Learners motivated by
interest in subject e.g.
local history, catering,
crafts, DIY

Learning supported
through LLN content

Learning and
achievement in
host subject

Learning and
achievement
LLN content

Discrete subject
learning

Further embedded
Learning

Discrete
LLN Learning

Move On

Move On is a national approach to supporting achievement of the national Certificate in Adult Literacy or Adult Numeracy. It aims to encourage those who need a 'brush-up' of literacy or numeracy skills.

"The Move On approach has a positive sell. It trains recruiters, anyone in touch with this brush-up group – IAG, Jobcentre Plus Advisers, teachers of any subject, Union Learning Reps, other learners, playgroup leaders and prison officers."
(www.move-on.org.uk)

13 Further challenges

Funding

Support for the delivery of embedded LLN is available via the LSC funding methodology. However, the current guidance, published in May 2004, reports,

> "In 2003-4, the LSC and the Adult Basic Skills Strategy Unit in the DfES co-funded an action research programme to look at a range of issues relating to embedded basic skills. The project report will be available on the LSC's website in summer 2004, together with further guidance on funding and recording embedded provision."
> (LSC, 2004a, p100)

Special LSC funds such as Basic Skills in Local Communities have also been successfully accessed. The DfES's Adult and Community Learning Fund has been used to develop and try out approaches to embedding LLN. Local LSCs have also made funds available to test and develop provision. Using such additional sources has enabled many organisations, from different sectors, to experiment and discover what seems to work best for them. They have then used more mainstream funds to sustain the work. Some organisations have used European funding to develop LLN whilst others have used additional sources from such initiatives as Sure Start. Funds from other government departments such as the Home Office and Health Authorities have also been accessed.

Working through different funding routes can be particularly challenging for voluntary and community learning providers as well as small- and medium-sized workplace providers. The challenge for most organisations is to fund the additional time that is required for staff teams to plan and work together. However, where embedding LLN is effective in motivating and supporting learning, retention and achievement should improve. It can be argued that higher retention and achievement should optimise funding, so the additional investment of time can be justified. Convincing organisations of such strategies can be challenging.

Staff qualifications

Where vocational staff have undertaken training in LLN, embedded models of delivery are more likely to be effective and long-lasting. Where LLN staff have spent time learning about the subject areas in which the LLN is embedded, the tuition offered to learners and the support offered to staff is more likely to be relevant and purposeful. Such strategies demand that staff can see the purposes and benefits of embedding LLN. Time, commitment and energy are required in an environment of competing and changing demand, initiatives and requirements. Some organisations have chosen to offer financial incentives to staff who take up LLN qualifications. This demonstrates a clear commitment to embedding LLN and recognises the investment required. At a time when there is clear commitment, by the government, to professional development in LLN learning, both opportunities and challenges arise.

Effectiveness

While acknowledgement has been made that embedded literacy, language and numeracy is desirable, further study and research is needed to demonstrate its effectiveness. Many practitioners, providers and policy makers feel that it is a sensible approach but further research into how learners feel they are learning and achieving in both their chosen subjects and LLN must be undertaken.

Richard Olivier

14 Check it out

For learners:

- Embedding LLN harnesses the natural ways in which we use these skills in every day living and working.
- Embedding LLN supports the reasons and purposes for which learners and potential learners want to engage in learning.
- Embedding LLN can be motivational, especially for those learners who would not take part in discreet LLN provision.
- Learners should know that their learning activity includes LL or N but that the content will be linked closely to their main or 'host' subject.
- Learners should receive assessment of the LLN skills needed to successfully complete their programme but this should be carried out sensitively and over a period of time.
- Learners' learning plans and reviews should cover both the host subject and the LLN content.
- Learners should be supported to identify progress and achievement in both areas of learning.

For providers:

- Whole organisational approaches to embedding LLN, supports learners and staff and provides wider progression opportunities.
- Models and approaches to embedding should be designed to address the interests, purposes and motivations of the learners.
- All organisations can adopt an embedded approach.
- Promotion and publicity materials should clearly state that LLN is included in the learning activity.
- The LLN infrastructure, including screening, assessment, individual learning plans and recording of achievement should be used.
- Close liaison between host subject staff and LLN staff should continue from the outset to the completion of the programme.
- Team teaching or teaching advice/consultancy should be a feature of an embedded approach to teaching LLN.
- Staff should be aware of the specialist knowledge and skills of both teaching areas; consideration should be given to staff gaining further qualifications.

- Mapping a host subject to the LLN standards and core curricula is not the same as embedding. Mapping is the beginning of the process.
- Progression opportunities should be identified prior to the delivery of the programme.
- Information, advice and guidance should be offered to support learners' progression.
- Recognition of achievement through records, accreditation or qualifications should be planned and discussed with learners from the outset.

Challenges:

- Embedding LLN is challenging, complex and time-consuming.
- Embedding requires high levels of co-operation between 'host' subject teachers and LLN teachers.
- Time to develop relationships, trust and understanding between staff is vital to successful embedding.
- Mutual recognition of the skills and knowledge of both the 'host' subject and LLN is required.
- Learners' purposes, motivations and reasons for engaging in the 'host' subject must be paramount. The LLN content must closely link to these, providing respect and integrity.
- It is easy to get carried away with the delivery of the host subject and forget to teach, assess and record progress in the associated LLN. However, where the two areas are closely synchronised, retention and achievement improves and the purposes of LLN learning become clearer.
- Mainstream funding to support embedding approaches remains unclear; additional sources of funding often need to be found to support the additional time required.
- As with all LLN provision, information, advice and guidance about progression opportunities can be a neglected area. It should be built into provision from the outset so that learners have optimum choices available.

Glossary

<u>Adult and Community Learning Fund (ACLF)</u> A Government initiative from 1998–2004 to support developmental projects designed to widen participation in adult learning.

<u>Adult Literacy Campaign</u> A Government-sponsored initiative of the early 1970s to promote literacy learning for adults.

<u>Common Inspection Framework (CIF)</u> The standards against which inspectors' judgements are made about the quality of adult learning.

<u>Contextualised literacy, language and numeracy</u> Where LLN is the primary learning goal but where teaching and learning draw on interests, purposes and needs of individuals or groups.

<u>English for Speakers of Other Languages (ESOL)</u> Where English is taught as a second or further language, for people who are resident in the UK.

<u>English for Specific Purposes (ESP)</u> English is taught for a specific work-related or interest-related purpose.

<u>English as a Foreign Language (EFL)</u> English is taught as a second or further language, for people who are either visiting the UK or who are resident in their home country and wish to learn English.

<u>Formative reviews</u> Reviews between learners and teachers which are held regularly during the learning programme, to reflect on and record progress and achievements.

<u>Fourth basic skill – ICT</u> In *21st Century Skills: Realising Our Potential* (DfES 2003), it was suggested that ICT should become an additional basic skill.

<u>Further Education Funding Council</u> The lead body for the funding of post-compulsory education from 1992–2001.

<u>Goals</u> Statements which capture what groups or individuals want to do as a result of being involved in learning. This might include further learning, volunteering, community involvement or paid employment.

<u>Learning outcomes</u> What a learner has gained in knowledge, skills or attitudes, for example, increased confidence. Learning outcomes may not be measured by formal assessment or tests.

<u>Move On</u> A national approach to supporting achievement of the national certificate in Adult Literacy or Numeracy.

<u>Planning learning and recording progress and achievement: a guide for practitioners</u> (DfES, 2004) A publication to offer detailed guidance to practitioners on best ways to plan learning, record progress and record achievement, produced by DfES working with LSDA.

<u>Progression routes</u> Learning pathways between different levels of learning or between different learning environments.

<u>Recognising and recording progress and achievement (RARPA)</u> An initiative to offer detailed guidance to practitioners on best ways to recognise and record progress and achievement in non-accredited learning.

<u>Skills for Life</u> The national strategy for improving adult literacy and numeracy skills has a target to improve the skills of 1.5million adults by 2007.

<u>SMOG</u> A guide to calculating word and sentence length to ensure the right level of readability of text.

<u>Summative reviews</u> are held at the end of a programme or a module of learning. They reflect on achievements on the completed learning activities and record future plans and aspirations.

<u>Targets</u> Short-term objectives that form building blocks of learning activity which help learners to achieve their goals.

References and further reading

Basic Skills Agency (2003) *Reaching Out with Basic Skills; a practical guide to community-focused basic skills work with socially excluded groups*, London, BSA

Department for Education and Employment (1999) *Improving Literacy and Numeracy: A fresh start*, Report of the working group chaired by Moser, C. Suffolk, DfEE

DfEE (2001) *Skills for Life, The national strategy for improving adult literacy and numeracy skills*, Nottingham, DfEE

DfEE (2002) *Success in Adult Literacy, Numeracy and ESOL Provision, A guide to support the Common Inspection Framework*, Nottingham, DfEE

DfES (2002) *A guide to the National Tests in Adult Literacy and Numeracy*, Nottingham, DfES

DfES (2003) *Case Study: Rodbaston College, Staffordshire*, Nottingham, DfES

DfES (2003) *The Skills for Life Teaching Qualifications Framework: A User's Guide*, Nottingham, DfES

DfES (2004) *Planning learning and recording progress and achievement: a guide for practitioners*, Nottingham, DfES.

DfES (2004) *A Contextual Guide to support success in literacy, numeracy and ESOL provision: Embedded Learning (Consultation Document)*, Nottingham, DfES

Dearing Report (1996)

Further Education Funding Council (1998) *Key Skills in Further Education: Good Practice Report*, Coventry, FEFC

Green, M and Milbourne, L (1998) *Making Learning Support Work*, London, FEDA

Learning and Skills Council (2002) *Evaluation of the Basic Skills in Local Communities Report*, Coventry, LSC

Learning and Skills Council (2004) *Basic Skills in Local Communities, 2003–4, Final Report* (Unpublished)

Learning and Skills Council (2004a) *Funding Guidance for Further Education in 2004/05 Coventry*, LSC

Learning and Skills Development Agency (LSDA) (2003) *Integrating Key Skills and Basic Skills*, London, LSDA

NIACE et al (2001) *Voluntary and community Sector Basic Skills and ESOL Fund (VSF): Final Report*, Leicester, NIACE

NIACE (2003) *Developing Embedded Basic Skills*, Leicester, NIACE (unpublished)

Nicholls, S and Naish, J (1981) *A handbook for ESL tutors*, London, BBC

Rhoder, C and French, J (1995) 'Participant-generated text: a vehicle for workplace literacy' in *The Journal of Adolescent and Adult Literacy* Vol 39(2).

Useful organisations and websites for work in literacy, language and numeracy

Useful organisations

ABSSU	Adult Basic Skills Strategy Unit
ALI	Adult Learning Inspectorate
BSA	Basic Skills Agency
DfEE	Department for Education and Employment
DfES	Department for Education and Skills
FENTO	Further Education National Training Organisation
LSC	Learning and Skills Council
LSDA	Learning and Skills Development Agency
NIACE	National Institute of Adult Continuing Education
NRDC	National Research and Development Centre for adult literacy and numeracy
QCA	Qualifications and Curriculum Authority

Useful websites

- Adult Basic Skills Strategy Unit (ABSSU) at the Department for Education and Skills
  http://www.dfes.gov.uk/readwriteplus
- Adults Learning Mathematics
  http://www.alm-online.org
- Basic Skills Agency (BSA)
  http://www.basic-skills.co.uk
- Basic Skills for Inclusive Learning Project
  http://www.ctad.co.uk/basil
- Further Education National Training Organization (FENTO) – Basic Skills home page
  http://www.fento.ac.uk
- Learning and Skills Council (LSC) – the funding body for post-16 education
  http://www.lsc.gov.uk
- Learning and Skills Development Agency (LSDA) - Basic Skills pages
  http://www.lsda.org.uk/programmes/basicskills
- London Adult Numeracy Professional Development Centre
  http://www.lsbu.ac.uk/numeracy
- National Association for Numeracy and Mathematics in Colleges (NANAMIC) – professional organization for college teachers
  http://www.nanamic.org.uk

- National Research and Development Centre for Adult Literacy and Numeracy
  http://www.nrdc.org.uk
- National Institute for Adult Continuing Education (NIACE
  http://www.niace.org.uk
- Qualifications and Curriculum Authority – Basic Skills page
  http://www.qca.org.uk
- Readwriteplus
  http://www.dfes.gov.uk/readwriteplus/teachingandlearning
  http://www.dfes.gov.uk/readwriteplus/nosmapping
  (for mapping LLN to National Occupational Standards)
  http://www.dfes.gov.uk/readwriteplus/DiagnosticMaterials
  (for accessing diagnostic materials from milestones to Level 2)
- Training Adult Literacy, ESOL and Numeracy Teachers
  http://www.talent.ac.uk